PREPARATORY SET #1

RUDIMENTS EXAM SERIES

By Glory St. Germain ARCT RMT MYCC UMTC &
Shelagh McKibbon-U'Ren RMT UMTC

ULTIMATE MUSIC THEORY

GSG MUSIC

Enriching Lives Through Music Education

ISBN: 978-1-927641-00-2

The Ultimate Music Theory™ Program
Enriching Lives Through Music Education

The Ultimate Music Theory™ Workbooks & Answer Books Program includes:

UMT Rudiments Workbooks for Prep 1, Prep 2, Basic, Intermediate, Advanced & Complete
UMT Exam Series (Set #1 & Set #2) for Preparatory, Basic, Intermediate & Advanced

Supplemental Workbooks for PREP LEVEL, LEVELS 1 - 8 & COMPLETE LEVEL
UMT Supplemental Exam Series for LEVEL 5, LEVEL 6, LEVEL 7 & LEVEL 8

The Ultimate Music Theory Program is the *Way to Score Success* as UMT helps students prepare for nationally recognized theory examinations including the Royal Conservatory of Music.

 Library and Archives Canada Cataloguing in Publication. UMT Workbooks & Exam Series /Glory St. Germain & Shelagh McKibbon-U'Ren. Respect Copyright. All rights reserved. GlorylandPublishing.com

Ultimate Music Theory Rudiments Exam Series

GP - EPS1	ISBN: 978-1-927641-00-2	Preparatory Rudiments Exams Set #1
GP - EPS1A	ISBN: 978-1-927641-08-8	Preparatory Exams Answers Set #1
GP - EPS2	ISBN: 978-1-927641-01-9	Preparatory Rudiments Exams Set #2
GP - EPS2A	ISBN: 978-1-927641-09-5	Preparatory Exams Answers Set #2
GP - EBS1	ISBN: 978-1-927641-02-6	Basic Rudiments Exams Set #1
GP - EBS1A	ISBN: 978-1-927641-10-1	Basic Exams Answers Set #1
GP - EBS2	ISBN: 978-1-927641-03-3	Basic Rudiments Exams Set #2
GP - EBS2A	ISBN: 978-1-927641-11-8	Basic Exams Answers Set #2
GP - EIS1	ISBN: 978-1-927641-04-0	Intermediate Rudiments Exams Set #1
GP - EIS1A	ISBN: 978-1-927641-12-5	Intermediate Exams Answers Set #1
GP - EIS2	ISBN: 978-1-927641-05-7	Intermediate Rudiments Exams Set #2
GP - EIS2A	ISBN: 978-1-927641-13-2	Intermediate Exams Answers Set #2
GP - EAS1	ISBN: 978-1-927641-06-4	Advanced Rudiments Exams Set #1
GP - EAS1A	ISBN: 978-1-927641-14-9	Advanced Exams Answers Set #1
GP - EAS2	ISBN: 978-1-927641-07-1	Advanced Rudiments Exams Set #2
GP - EAS2A	ISBN: 978-1-927641-15-6	Advanced Exams Answers Set #2

Ultimate Music Theory Supplemental Exam Series

GP-L5E	ISBN: 978-1-990358-11-1	LEVEL 5 Exams
GP-L5EA	ISBN: 978-1-990358-12-8	LEVEL 5 Exams Answers
GP-L6E	ISBN: 978-1-990358-13-5	LEVEL 6 Exams
GP-L6EA	ISBN: 978-1-990358-14-2	LEVEL 6 Exams Answers
GP-L7E	ISBN: 978-1-990358-15-9	LEVEL 7 Exams
GP-L7EA	ISBN: 978-1-990358-16-6	LEVEL 7 Exams Answers
GP-L8E	ISBN: 978-1-990358-17-3	LEVEL 8 Exams
GP-L8EA	ISBN: 978-1-990358-18-0	LEVEL 8 Exams Answers

Go to UltimateMusicTheory.com and check out the FREE Resources

Ultimate Music Theory FREE RESOURCES created just for you!

The **Ultimate Music Theory Exams** reinforce the **UMT Prep 1 and Prep 2 Rudiments Workbooks** and prepare students for continued learning with UMT Basic Rudiments.

Preparatory Rudiments Theory Examination requirements are:

Pitch
- Grand Staff (Treble Clef or G Clef and Bass Clef or F Clef)
- Note names (up to two ledger lines below and above the Treble Clef and Bass Clef)
- Accidentals (sharp, flat and natural signs)
- Whole tones (whole steps) and semitones (half steps)
- Matching notes to the corresponding keys on the keyboard
- Naming or drawing notes on the staff that are shown on a keyboard

Rhythm
- Note and rest time values (whole, half, quarter and eighth)
- Dotted half notes and dotted quarter notes
- Adding Time Signatures, bar lines and rests to a given line of music
- Simple Time Signatures ($\frac{2}{4}$, $\frac{3}{4}$, $\frac{4}{4}$, and $\mathbf{C}$)

Scales in the keys of C Major, G Major and F Major
- Write or identify: Scales, ascending or descending, one octave
- Key Signatures
- Tonic scale degree

Triads in the keys of C Major, G Major and F Major
- Write or identify: Solid (blocked) in Root Position, beginning on the Tonic note (with or without a Key Signature)
- Identify: Broken in Root Position, beginning on the Tonic note (with or without a Key Signature)

Intervals
- Write or identify: above a given note, all intervals up to and including an octave (numerical size only), melodic or harmonic
- Identify: below a given note, all intervals up to and including an octave (numerical size only), melodic form only

Musical Terms and Signs
- Recognize, define or supply the musical terms or signs as listed in the Prep 1 and Prep 2 Ultimate Music Theory Workbooks

Analysis
- Analyze a short musical composition, identifying any of the above theory requirements

Score:
60 - 69 Pass; 70 - 79 Honors; 80 - 89 First Class Honors; 90 - 100 First Class Honors with Distinction

Ultimate Music Theory: *The Way to Score Success!*

UltimateMusicTheory.com © Copyright 2013 Gloryland Publishing. All Rights Reserved.

ULTIMATE MUSIC THEORY
PREPARATORY EXAM SET #1 - EXAM #1

Total Score: ____
100

♪ **UMT Tip:** When drawing a line from each note to the corresponding key on the keyboard, start with Middle C (or the note closest to Middle C).

1. Name the following notes. Draw a line from each note to the corresponding key on the keyboard (at the correct pitch).

___
10

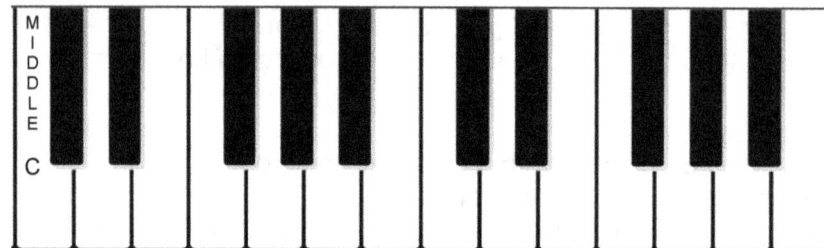

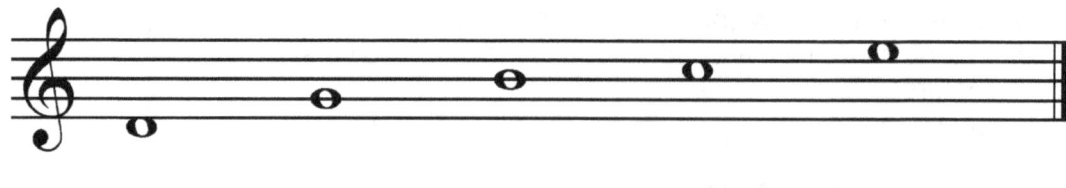

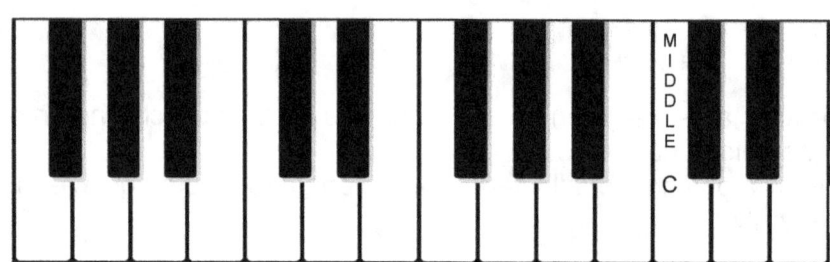

UltimateMusicTheory.com © Copyright 2013 Gloryland Publishing. All Rights Reserved.

ULTIMATE MUSIC THEORY
PREPARATORY EXAM SET #1 - EXAM #1

> ♪ **UMT Tip:** Draw a small keyboard at the bottom of the page. For each pair of notes, find them on the keyboard. Identify which note is at the higher pitch (to the right of the keyboard).

2. For each pair of notes, circle the note which sounds HIGHER in pitch.

[10]

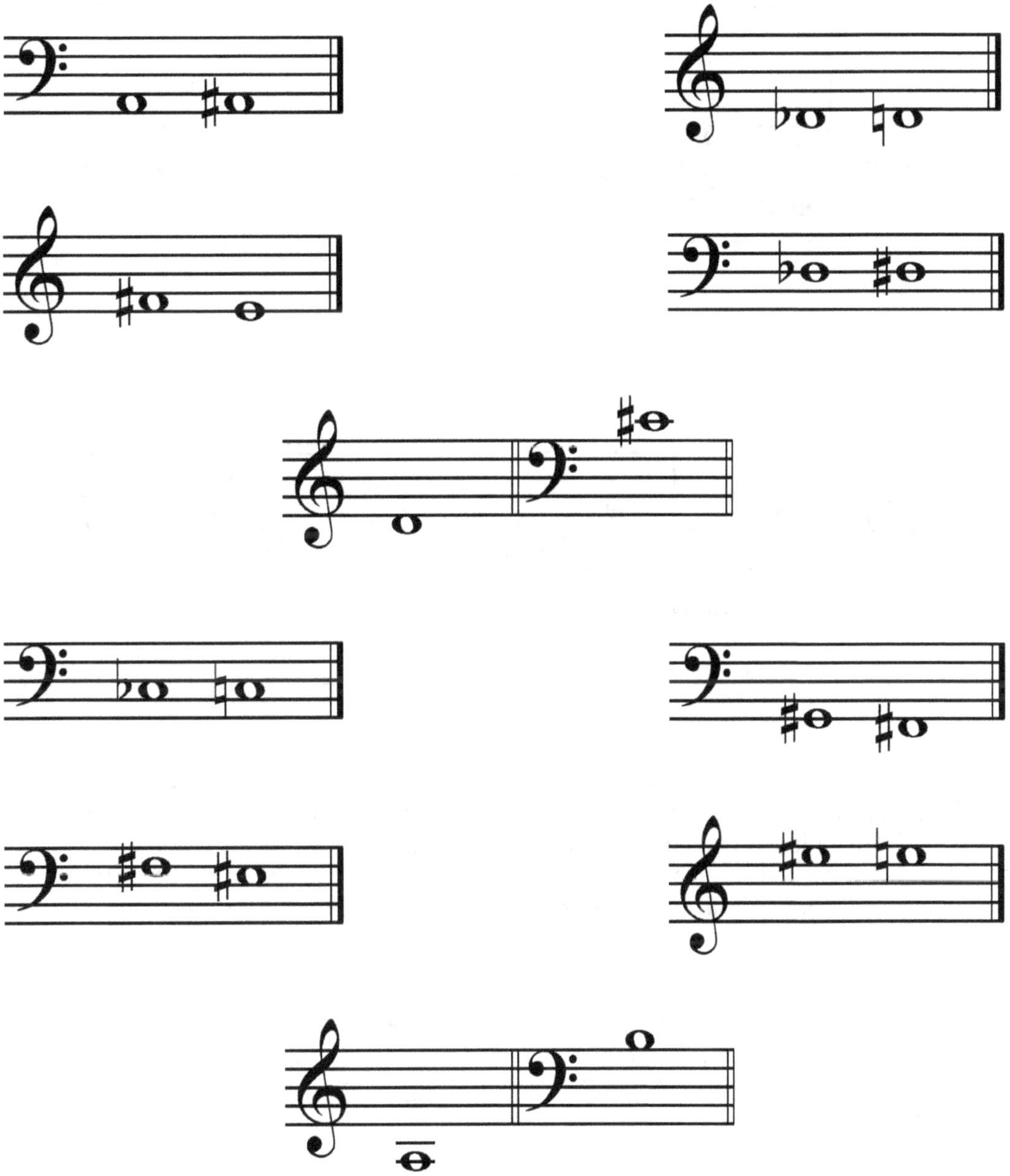

ULTIMATE MUSIC THEORY
PREPARATORY EXAM SET #1 - EXAM #1

> ♪ **UMT Tip:** Count the lines and spaces from the lower (bottom) note to the higher (upper) note. The lower (bottom) note is always counted as "1".
> OR
> Name the notes. Count the number of letter names from the lower (bottom) note to the higher (upper) note. The lower (bottom) note is always counted as "1".

3. a) Name the interval size for each boxed interval. (Write the number size only.)

> ♪ **UMT Tip:** A harmonic interval is written one note above the other. A harmonic 1st and a harmonic 2nd are written one note beside the other (touching).

b) Write the following harmonic intervals above the given notes. Use whole notes.

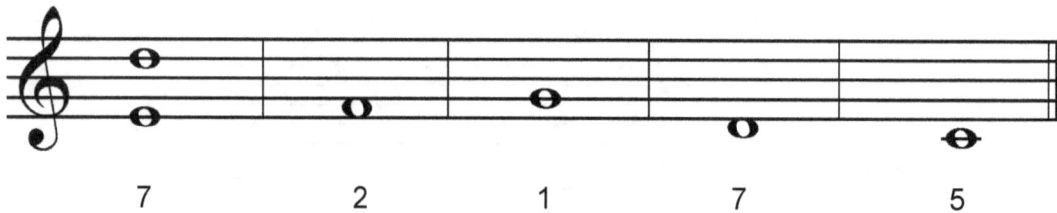

ULTIMATE MUSIC THEORY
PREPARATORY EXAM SET #1 - EXAM #1

> ♪ **UMT Tip:** When using a Key Signature, the Key Signature must be written before the scale starts. Do not start the scale underneath the Key Signature.

4. Write the following scales. Use whole notes.

    ___
    10

   a) The scale of G Major, ascending (going up) one octave. Use a Key Signature. Circle one Tonic note. Label it as **I**.

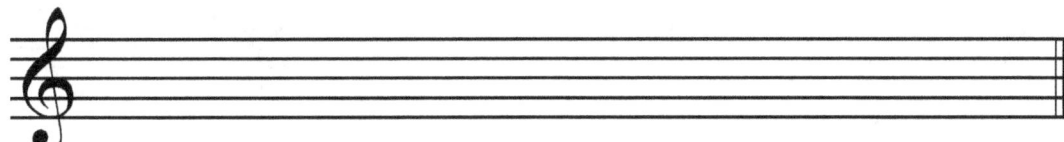

   b) The scale of F Major, descending (going down) one octave. Use a Key Signature. Circle one Tonic note. Label it as **I**.

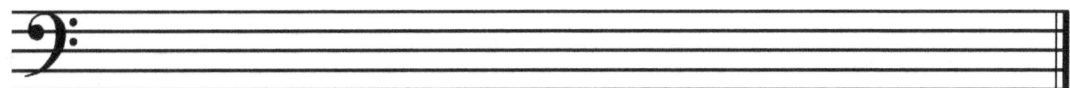

   c) The scale of C Major, descending (going down) one octave, beginning on the given note.

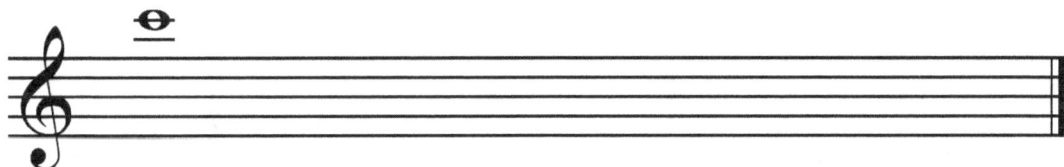

   d) The scale of C Major, ascending (going up) one octave, beginning on the given note.

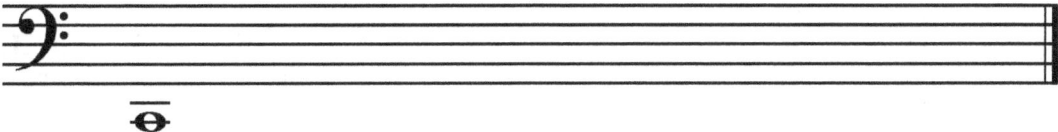

ULTIMATE MUSIC THEORY
PREPARATORY EXAM SET #1 - EXAM #1

> ♪ **UMT Tip:** Identify whether the triad is written in the Treble Clef or in the Bass Clef. Write the name of the root note below each triad. Use this to help you match each triad name with the correct triad.

5. Match each triad name with the correct triad.

___
10

TRIAD NAME		**TRIAD**
C Major triad, solid, in the Bass Clef	b)	a)
C Major triad, broken, in the Treble Clef	___	b) root note: C
G Major triad, solid, in the Treble Clef	___	c)
G Major triad, solid, in the Bass Clef	___	d)
F Major triad, broken, in the Bass Clef	___	e)
F Major triad, broken, in the Treble Clef	___	f)

UltimateMusicTheory.com © Copyright 2013 Gloryland Publishing. All Rights Reserved.

ULTIMATE MUSIC THEORY
PREPARATORY EXAM SET #1 - EXAM #1

♪ **UMT Tip:** Write the value below each note and rest.

6. a) Draw a line to connect each rest with the note that has the same value.

   b) Name the following notes.

   two (beamed) eighth notes
   _____
   _____
   _____
   _____
   _____
   _____

ULTIMATE MUSIC THEORY
PREPARATORY EXAM SET #1 - EXAM #1

> ♪ **UMT Tip:** A quarter note equals one Basic Beat. Scoop each Basic Beat in each measure.

7. a) Write the correct Time Signature below each bracket.

> ♪ **UMT Tip:** Bar lines start at the top of the staff and end at the bottom of the staff. They are not written outside of the staff. Use a ruler to draw bar lines.

b) Add bar lines to complete the following rhythms.

ULTIMATE MUSIC THEORY
PREPARATORY EXAM SET #1 - EXAM #1

♪ **UMT Tip:** Write the value below each note and rest.

8. a) Draw one note that is equal in value to the combined value of the given notes.

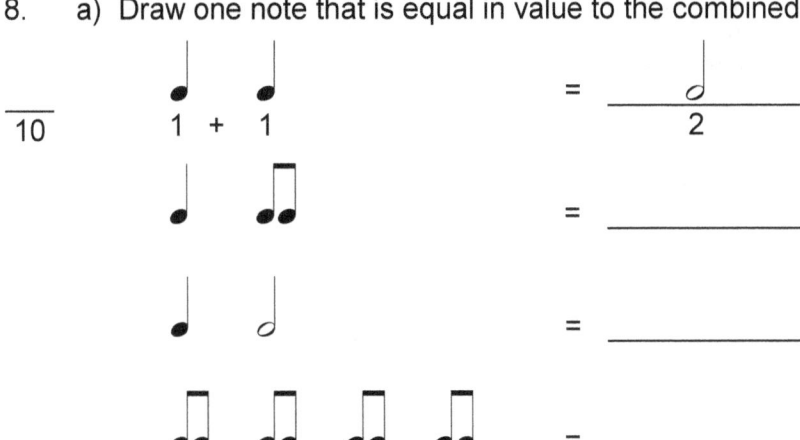

b) Draw one rest that is equal in value to the combined value of the given rests.

ULTIMATE MUSIC THEORY
PREPARATORY EXAM SET #1 - EXAM #1

> ♪ **UMT Tip:** Before looking at the possible definitions, look at the Italian Term and identify the definition. Then select the matching definition from one of the two choices.

9. Circle the correct definition for each Italian term.

Italian Term

___
10

Term	a)	b)
tempo	**a) speed (fast or slow)** ⭕	b) volume (loud or soft)
staccato	a) detached	b) smooth
largo	a) very loud	b) very slow
a tempo	a) return to the original tempo	b) play at a faster tempo
ritardando	a) slowing down gradually	b) getting faster quickly
moderato	a) very fast	b) at a moderate tempo
piano	a) loud	b) soft
allegro	a) slow	b) fast
mezzo piano	a) moderately soft	b) moderately slow
diminuendo	a) becoming softer	b) becoming louder
dynamics	a) volume (loud or soft)	b) pitch (high or low)

ULTIMATE MUSIC THEORY
PREPARATORY EXAM SET #1 - EXAM #1

> ♪ **UMT Tip:** The Time Signature must go under the bracket in the Treble Clef **and** in the Bass Clef.

10. Analyze the following piece of music by answering the questions below.

Purple Jelly Beans

Allegro   S. McKibbon

a) Name the title of this piece. _____

b) Name the composer of this piece. _____

c) Add the Time Signature directly on the music.

d) Explain the meaning of "*mf*". _____

e) Name the interval at **A** (number size only). _____

f) Name the interval at **B** (number size only). _____

g) Circle the name of the triad at the letter **C**.   C Major   F Major   G Major

h) Circle the name of the symbol at the letter **D**.   slur   staccato   fermata

i) Circle and name the highest note in this piece. _____

j) When the repeat sign is followed, how many measures are played? _____

UltimateMusicTheory.com © Copyright 2013 Gloryland Publishing. All Rights Reserved.

ULTIMATE MUSIC THEORY
PREPARATORY EXAM SET #1 - EXAM #2

Total Score: ____ / 100

> ♪ **UMT Tip:** When drawing a line from each note to the corresponding key on the keyboard, start with Middle C (or the note closest to Middle C). Notes in the Bass Clef will be below Middle C (to the left of Middle C on the keyboard). Notes in the Treble Clef will be above Middle C (to the right of Middle C on the keyboard).

1. a) Name the following notes. Draw a line from each note to the corresponding key on the keyboard (at the correct pitch).

10

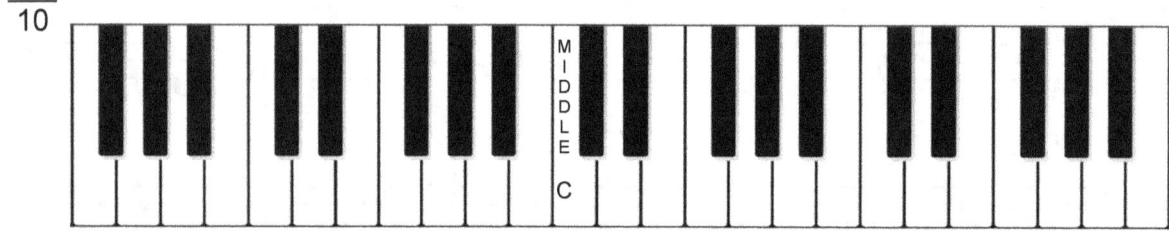

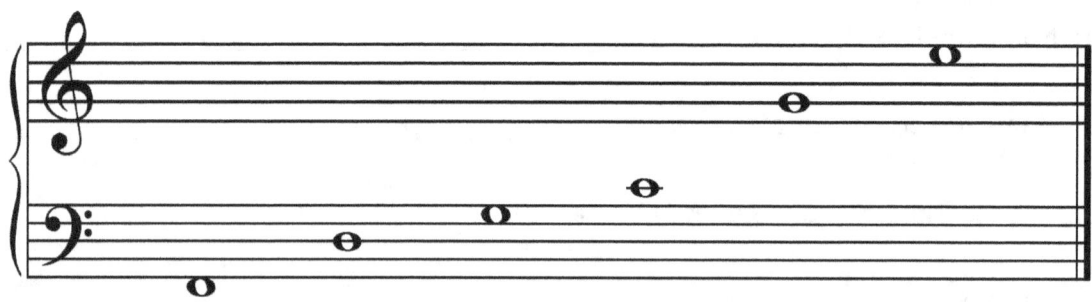

____ ____ ____ ____ ____

> ♪ **UMT Tip:** Accidentals are written before the note and after the letter name. An accidental is cancelled by another accidental or by a bar line.

b) Name the following notes.

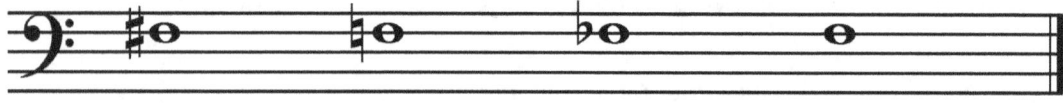

____ ____ ____ ____

UltimateMusicTheory.com © Copyright 2013 Gloryland Publishing. All Rights Reserved.

ULTIMATE MUSIC THEORY
PREPARATORY EXAM SET #1 - EXAM #2

> ♪ **UMT Tip:** Draw a small keyboard at the bottom of the page. For each pair of notes, find them on the keyboard and identify which note is at the lower pitch (on the left/bottom).

2. a) For each pair of notes, circle the note which sounds LOWER in pitch.

[10]

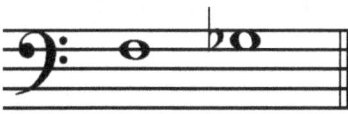

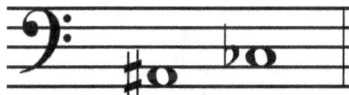

> ♪ **UMT Tip:** Use the keyboard that you drew at the bottom of the page. For each pair of notes, find them on the keyboard and identify the distance as either a semitone or a whole tone.

b) Name each of the following intervals as ST (semitone or half step) or as WT (whole tone or whole step).

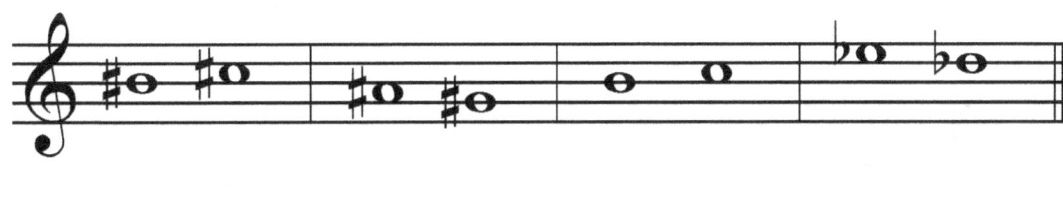

_____   _____   _____   _____

UltimateMusicTheory.com © Copyright 2013 Gloryland Publishing. All Rights Reserved.

ULTIMATE MUSIC THEORY
PREPARATORY EXAM SET #1 - EXAM #2

> ♪ **UMT Tip:** Count the lines and spaces from the lower (bottom) note to the higher (upper) note. The lower (bottom) note is always counted as "1".
> OR
> Name the notes. Count the number of letter names from the lower (bottom) note to the higher (upper) note. The lower (bottom) note is always counted as "1".

3. a) Name the interval size for each boxed interval. (Write the number size only.)

[10]

> ♪ **UMT Tip:** A harmonic interval is written one note above the other. A harmonic 1st and a harmonic 2nd are written one note beside the other (touching).

b) Write the following harmonic intervals above the given notes. Use whole notes.

    6   1   7   4   2

ULTIMATE MUSIC THEORY
PREPARATORY EXAM SET #1 - EXAM #2

> ♪ **UMT Tip:** When writing a scale going up or down one octave, the Tonic note is the first note and the last (final) note. The Roman Numeral "**I**" is used to label the Tonic note.

4. a) Write the scale of G Major, descending (going down) one octave. Use accidentals instead of a Key Signature. Use whole notes. Circle one Tonic note. Label it as **I**.

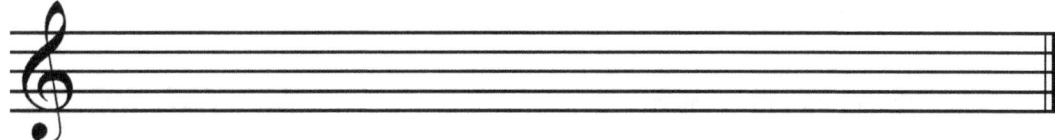

b) Write the scale of F Major, ascending (going up) one octave. Use accidentals instead of a Key Signature. Use whole notes. Circle one Tonic note. Label it as **I**.

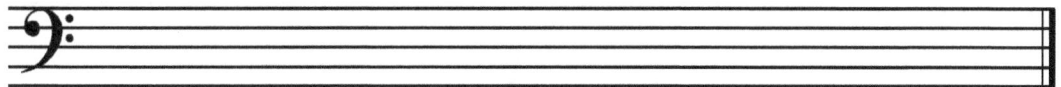

c) Add a Treble Clef or a Bass Clef at the beginning of the following staff to form the C Major Scale (ascending).

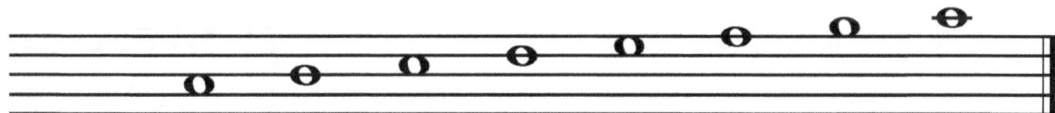

d) Write the Key Signature and the Tonic note for each of the following keys. Use whole notes.

G Major   F Major

UltimateMusicTheory.com © Copyright 2013 Gloryland Publishing. All Rights Reserved.

ULTIMATE MUSIC THEORY
PREPARATORY EXAM SET #1 - EXAM #2

> ♪ **UMT Tip:** A solid (blocked) triad is written one note above the other (all 3 notes on lines or all 3 notes in spaces). The root (lowest/bottom) note is the Tonic note.

5. Write the following solid (blocked) triads in root position beginning on the Tonic note. Use whole notes.

__
10

TRIAD NAME	TRIAD
a) Tonic triad of C Major in the Treble Clef	
b) Tonic triad of C Major in the Bass Clef	
c) Tonic triad of G Major in the Treble Clef	
d) Tonic triad of G Major in the Bass Clef	
e) Tonic triad of F Major in the Bass Clef	
f) Tonic triad of F Major in the Treble Clef	

UltimateMusicTheory.com © Copyright 2013 Gloryland Publishing. All Rights Reserved.

ULTIMATE MUSIC THEORY
PREPARATORY EXAM SET #1 - EXAM #2

> ♪ **UMT Tip:** In $\frac{4}{4}$ time, a quarter note equals one count.

6. a) Draw the following rests. Indicate the number of counts each rest receives in $\frac{4}{4}$ time.

   10

   Whole rest   _____   Number of counts: _____

   Quarter rest   _____   Number of counts: _____

   Eighth rest   _____   Number of counts: _____

   Half rest   _____   Number of counts: _____

   b) Draw the following notes. Indicate the number of counts each note receives in $\frac{4}{4}$ time.

   Half note   _____   Number of counts: _____

   (Single) Eighth note   _____   Number of counts: _____

   Whole note   _____   Number of counts: _____

   Dotted quarter note   _____   Number of counts: _____

   Quarter note   _____   Number of counts: _____

   Dotted half note   _____   Number of counts: _____

UltimateMusicTheory.com © Copyright 2013 Gloryland Publishing. All Rights Reserved.

ULTIMATE MUSIC THEORY
PREPARATORY EXAM SET #1 - EXAM #2

> ♪ **UMT Tip:** A quarter note equals one beat. Scoop the beats. Write the Basic Beat and pulse below each measure. Cross off the Basic Beat as each beat is completed.

7. a) Add rests below each bracket to complete each measure.

> ♪ **UMT Tip:** Bar lines start at the top of the staff and end at the bottom of the staff. They are not written outside of the staff. Use a ruler to draw bar lines.

b) Add bar lines to complete the following rhythms.

ULTIMATE MUSIC THEORY
PREPARATORY EXAM SET #1 - EXAM #2

> ♪ **UMT Tip:** Write the value below each note and rest. Add the numbers together to give you the value of the note or rest that you need to draw.

8. a) Draw one note that is equal in value to the combined value of the given notes.

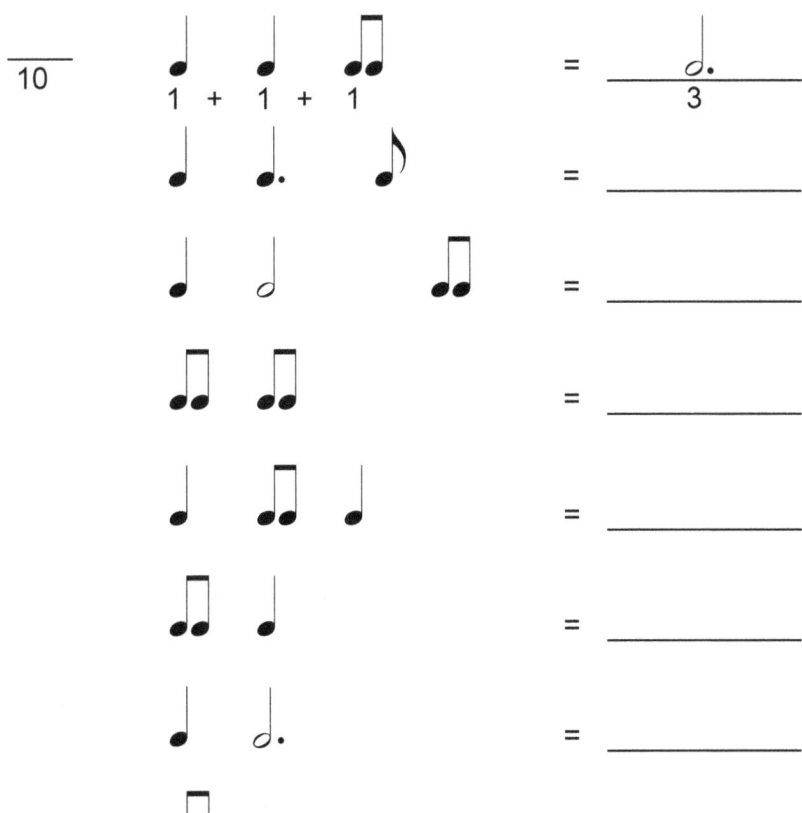

b) Draw one rest that is equal in value to the combined value of the given rests.

ULTIMATE MUSIC THEORY
PREPARATORY EXAM SET #1 - EXAM #2

> ♪ **UMT Tip:** Dynamic signs indicate how loud or soft to play. Write the definitions (dynamic level) for each dynamic sign first.

9. a) List the following dynamic signs in order from softest to loudest.

   Dynamic Signs:

   mf   *mp*   *f*   *p*   *ff*   *pp*

   _____ _____ _____ _____ _____ _____

   (softest)   (loudest)

   b) Write the musical sign for the following Terms. (Use signs, not abbreviations.)

   Terms:

   crescendo _____

   decrescendo _____

   fermata _____

   diminuendo _____

ULTIMATE MUSIC THEORY
PREPARATORY EXAM SET #1 - EXAM #2

♪ **UMT Tip:** The Key Signature affects every note on the staff (including on ledger lines) with the same letter name.

10. Analyze the following piece of music by answering the questions below.

Tadpole's Waltz

Allegro S. McKibbon

a) Name the title of this piece. _____

b) Name the tempo of this piece. _____

c) Add the Time Signature directly on the music.

d) Explain the meaning of "f". _____

e) Name the interval at **A** (number size only). _____

f) Name the notes at the letters **B**: _____ **C**: _____

g) Name the interval at **D** (number size only). _____

h) Add the correct rest in the Bass Clef in measure 2.

i) How many times is the note F♯ played in this piece? _____

j) How many measures are in this piece? _____

ULTIMATE MUSIC THEORY
PREPARATORY EXAM SET #1 - EXAM #3

Total Score: ___ / 100

1. a) Write the notes on the Grand Staff for the keys marked with a ☺. Use whole notes.
    b) Name the notes.
    c) Draw a line from each note to the corresponding key on the keyboard (at the correct pitch).

/10

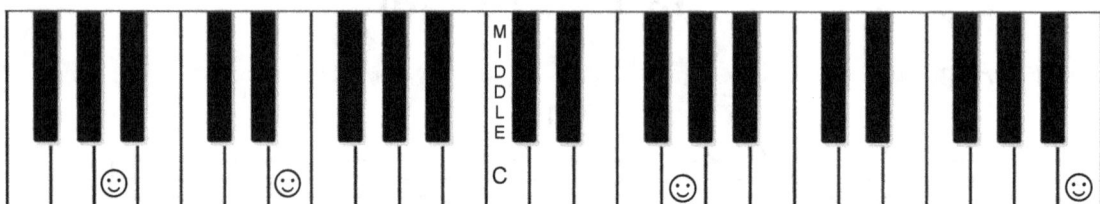

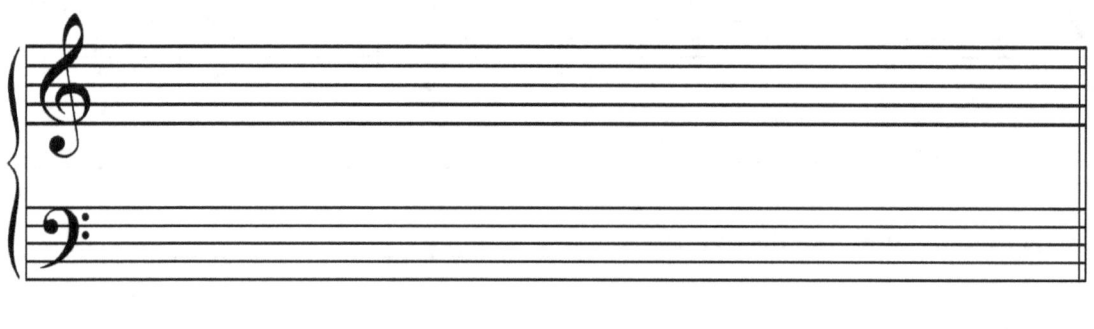

d) Name the following notes.

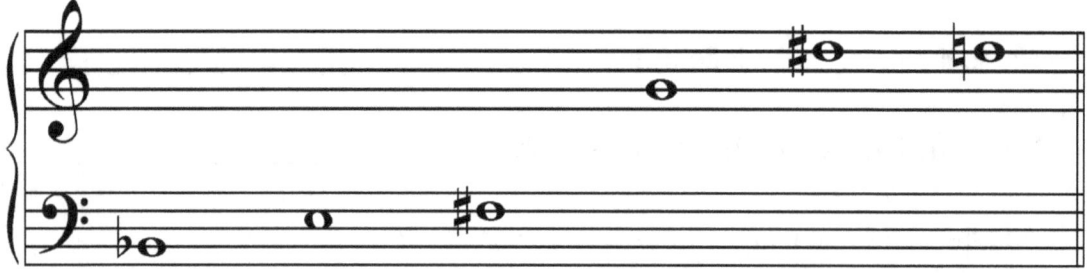

UltimateMusicTheory.com © Copyright 2013 Gloryland Publishing. All Rights Reserved.

ULTIMATE MUSIC THEORY
PREPARATORY EXAM SET #1 - EXAM #3

2. a) For each pair of notes, circle the note which sounds lower in pitch. Name the notes.

___
10

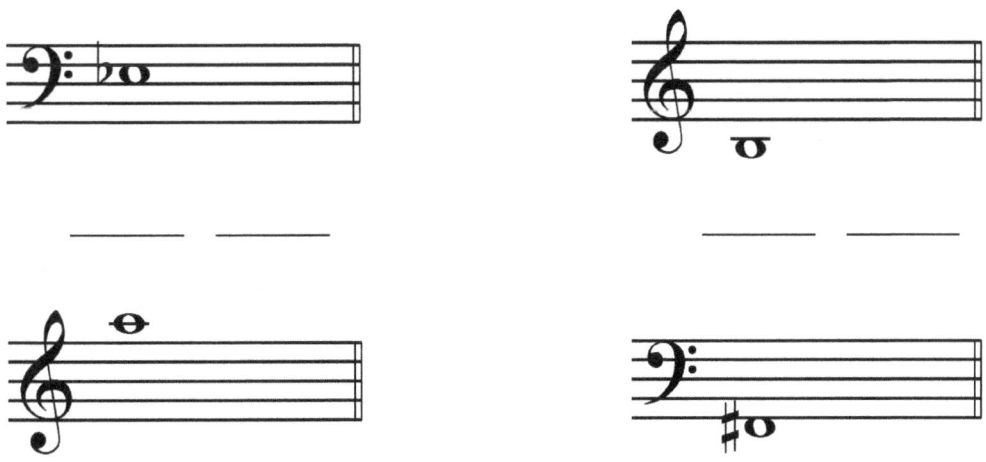

b) Beside each note, write the note that is one whole tone (whole step) higher. Use whole notes. Name the notes.

ULTIMATE MUSIC THEORY
PREPARATORY EXAM SET #1 - EXAM #3

3. a) Name the interval at each of the following letters. (Write the number size only.)

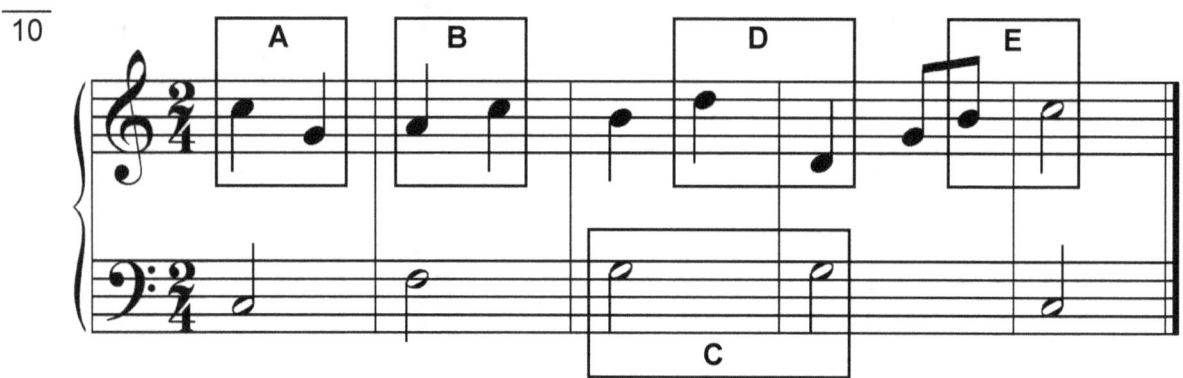

A _____

B _____

C _____

D _____

E _____

b) Write a note above each of the given notes to form the following harmonic intervals. Use whole notes.

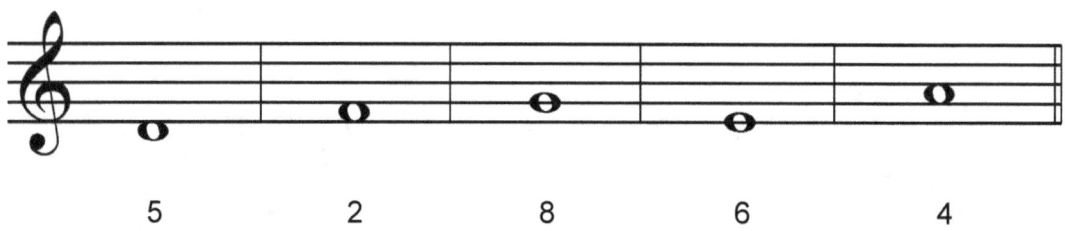

ULTIMATE MUSIC THEORY
PREPARATORY EXAM SET #1 - EXAM #3

4. Indicate if the rests in each measure are correct or incorrect by circling either CORRECT or INCORRECT.

      CORRECT   CORRECT   CORRECT

      INCORRECT   INCORRECT   INCORRECT

      CORRECT   CORRECT

      INCORRECT   INCORRECT

      CORRECT   CORRECT

      INCORRECT   INCORRECT

      CORRECT   CORRECT   CORRECT

      INCORRECT   INCORRECT   INCORRECT

ULTIMATE MUSIC THEORY
PREPARATORY EXAM SET #1 - EXAM #3

5. a) Write the scale of F Major, descending (going down) one octave. Use accidentals instead of a Key Signature. Use whole notes. Circle two Tonic notes. Label them **I**.

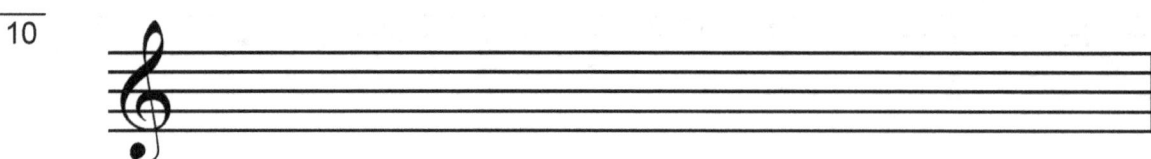

b) Write the scale of G Major, ascending (going up) one octave. Use accidentals instead of a Key Signature. Use whole notes. Circle two Tonic notes. Label them **I**.

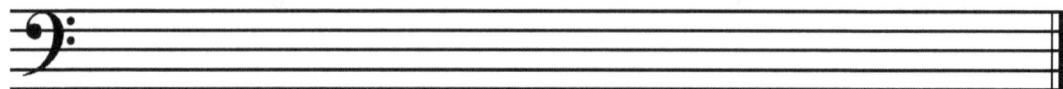

c) Add a Treble Clef or a Bass Clef at the beginning of the following staff to form the C Major Scale (descending).

d) Add a Treble Clef or a Bass Clef at the beginning of the following staff to form the C Major Scale (ascending).

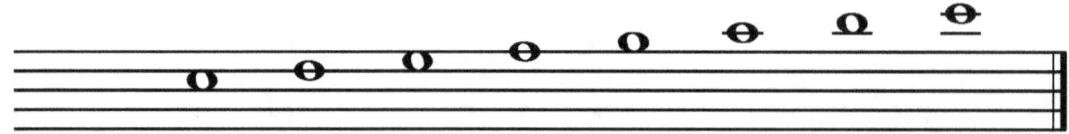

ULTIMATE MUSIC THEORY
PREPARATORY EXAM SET #1 - EXAM #3

6. Write the following solid (blocked) triads in Root Position on the Tonic note. Use whole notes.

__10__

G Major triad in the Bass Clef.
Use accidentals.

F Major triad in the Treble Clef.
Use a Key Signature.

C Major triad in the Bass Clef.
Use a Key Signature.

G Major triad in the Treble Clef.
Use a Key Signature.

F Major triad in the Bass Clef.
Use accidentals.

UltimateMusicTheory.com © Copyright 2013 Gloryland Publishing. All Rights Reserved.

ULTIMATE MUSIC THEORY
PREPARATORY EXAM SET #1 - EXAM #3

7. a) Draw a line from each rest to the note with the same value.

   b) Name the following notes and rests. Do not use abbreviations.

ULTIMATE MUSIC THEORY
PREPARATORY EXAM SET #1 - EXAM #3

8. a) Add bar lines to complete the following rhythms.

b) Add the correct Time Signature below each bracket.

ULTIMATE MUSIC THEORY
PREPARATORY EXAM SET #1 - EXAM #3

9. Circle the correct symbol or sign for each of the following definitions.

$\frac{}{10}$

Definition	Sign or Symbol		
detached	♩.	or	𝄐♩
moderately loud	*mp*	or	*mf*
lowers the note a semitone (half step)	♯	or	♭
becoming louder	>	or	<
loud	*f*	or	*p*
play the notes *legato*	♩♩♩	or	♩♩
becoming softer	*cresc.*	or	*decresc.*
cancels a sharp or a flat	♮	or	♯
indicates the end of a piece	═══	or	═══‖
raises a note one semitone (half step)	♯	or	♭

UltimateMusicTheory.com © Copyright 2013 Gloryland Publishing. All Rights Reserved.

ULTIMATE MUSIC THEORY
PREPARATORY EXAM SET #1 - EXAM #3

10. Analyze the following piece of music by answering the questions below.

Lia's Laugh

S. McKibbon

a) Name the title of this piece. _____

b) Explain the tempo of this piece. _____

c) Name the composer of this piece. _____

e) Name the Key of this piece. _____

d) Circle the correct name of the sign at **A**:   staccato   slur   tie   fermata

f) Circle the correct name of the sign at **B**:   staccato   slur   tie   fermata

g) Circle the correct name of the sign at **C**:   staccato   slur   tie   fermata

h) Add a tie between the notes in the Bass Clef at measures 2 and 3.

i) Name the notes at the letters: D _____   E _____   F _____

j) How many times is the note G played in this piece? _____

UltimateMusicTheory.com © Copyright 2013 Gloryland Publishing. All Rights Reserved.

ULTIMATE MUSIC THEORY
PREPARATORY EXAM SET #1 - EXAM #4

Total Score: ___ / 100

1. a) Write the notes on the Grand Staff for the keys marked with a ☺. Use whole notes.
   b) Name the notes.
   c) Draw a line from each note to the corresponding key on the keyboard (at the correct pitch).

   /10

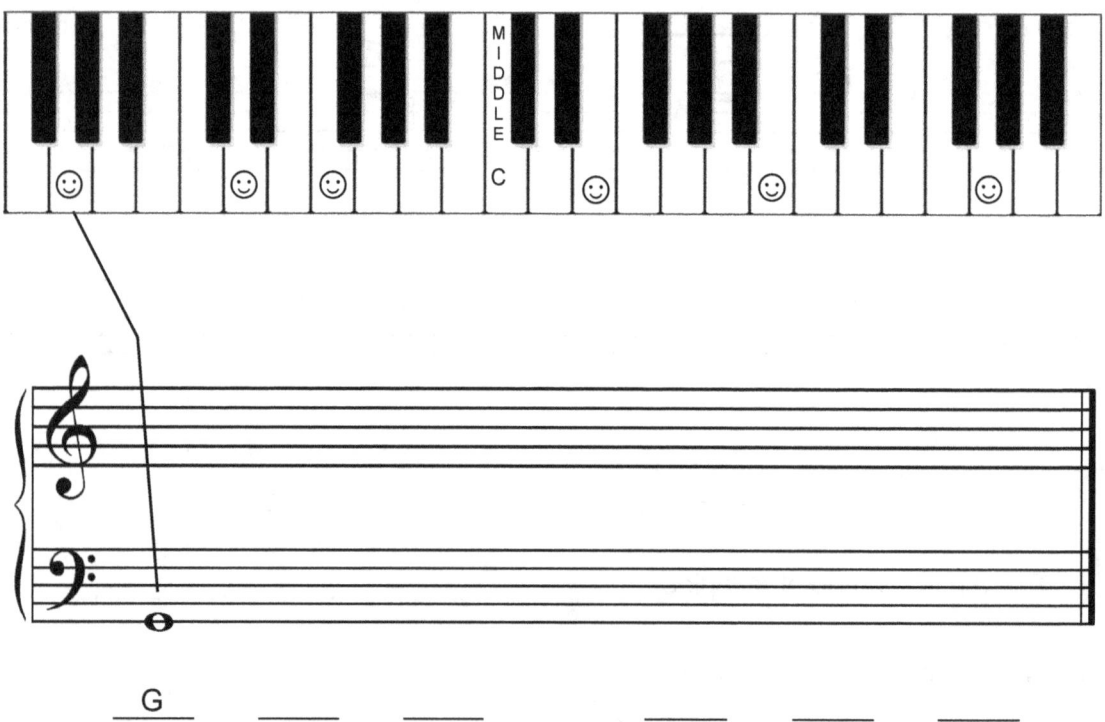

G ___ ___ ___ ___ ___

d) Name the following notes. (Observe the Key Signature.)

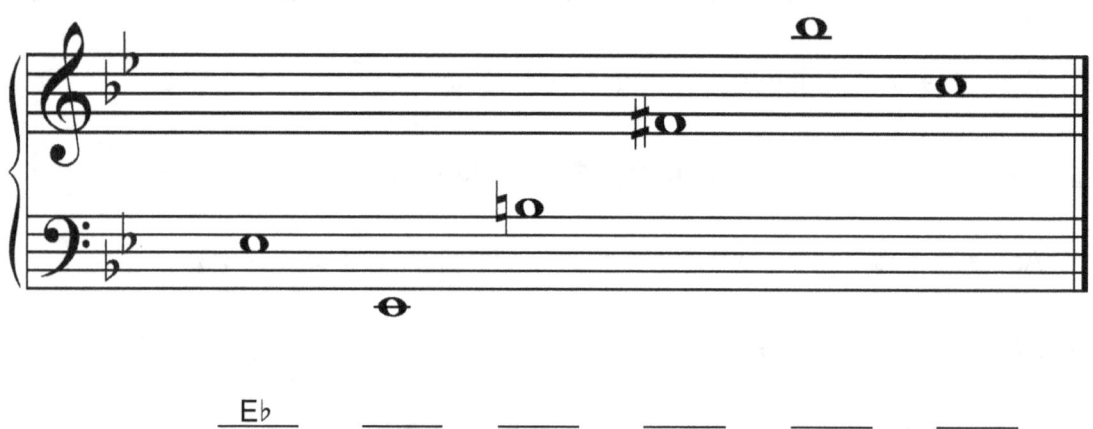

E♭ ___ ___ ___ ___ ___

ULTIMATE MUSIC THEORY
PREPARATORY EXAM SET #1 - EXAM #4

2. a) For each pair of notes, circle the note which sounds LOWER in pitch.

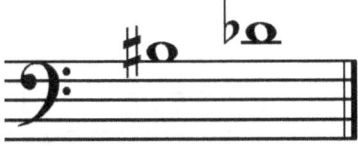

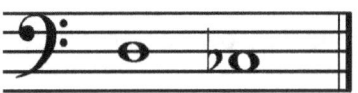

b) Beside each note, write the note that is one whole tone (whole step) higher. Use whole notes.

ULTIMATE MUSIC THEORY
PREPARATORY EXAM SET #1 - EXAM #4

3. a) Name each of the following melodic intervals. (Write the number size only.)

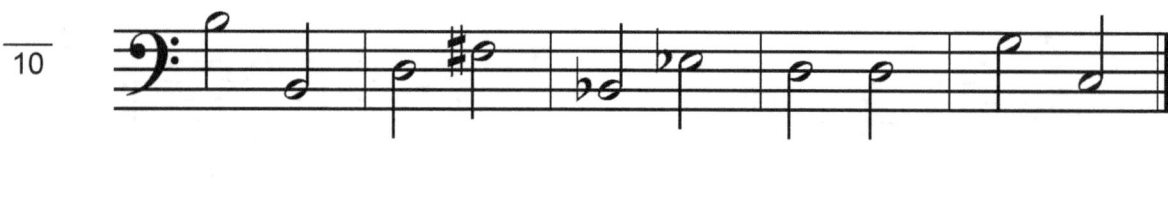

b) Write a note above each of the given notes to form the following harmonic intervals.

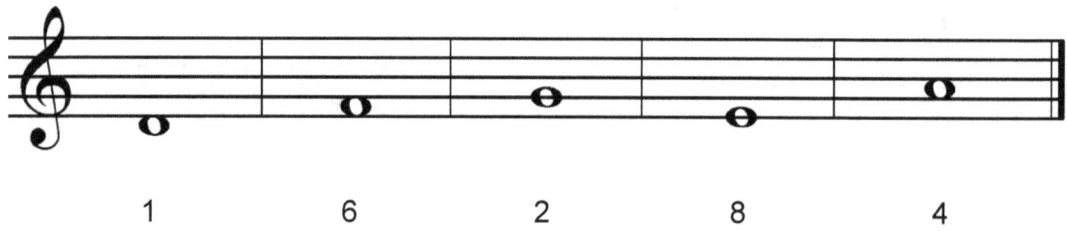

4. Add rests below each bracket to complete each measure.

ULTIMATE MUSIC THEORY
PREPARATORY EXAM SET #1 - EXAM #4

5. a) Write the scale of G Major, descending (going down) one octave. Use accidentals instead of a Key Signature. Use whole notes. Circle two Tonic notes. Label them I.

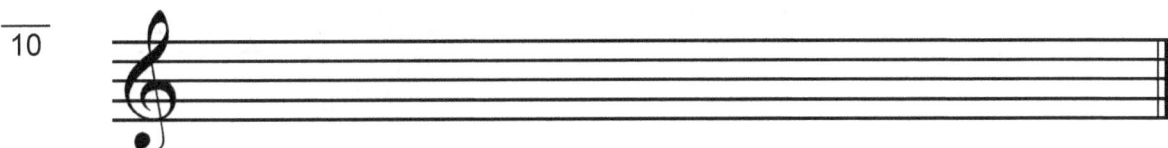

b) Write the scale of F Major, ascending (going up) one octave. Use accidentals instead of a Key Signature. Use whole notes. Circle two Tonic notes. Label them I.

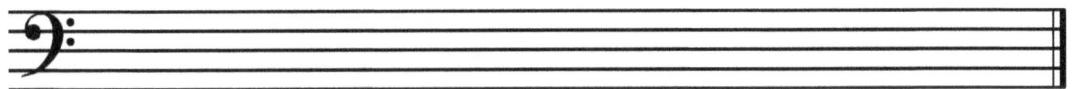

c) Add a Treble Clef or a Bass Clef at the beginning of the following staff to form the C Major Scale (descending).

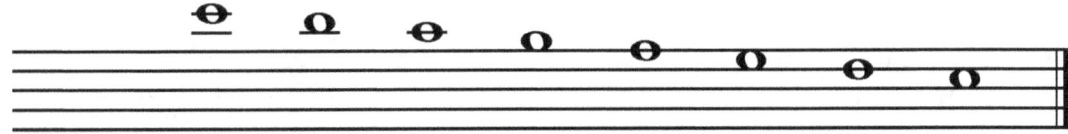

d) Write the Key Signature and the Tonic note for each of the following keys. Use whole notes.

ULTIMATE MUSIC THEORY
PREPARATORY EXAM SET #1 - EXAM #4

6. Match each triad name with the correct triad.

<u> </u>
10   G Major Triad, Broken,   d   a)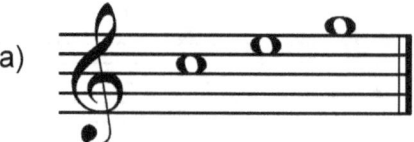
     in the Bass Clef

C Major Triad, Solid,   b)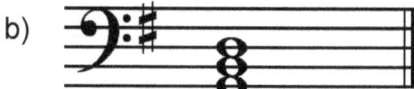
in the Treble Clef

G Major Triad, Solid,   c)
in the Bass Clef

C Major Triad, Broken,   d)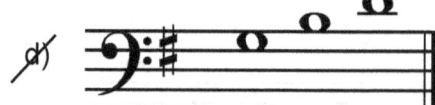
in the Treble Clef

F Major Triad, Solid,   e)
in the Bass Clef

F Major Triad, Broken,   f)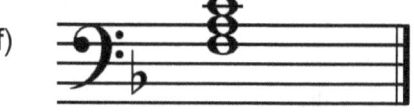
in the Treble Clef

ULTIMATE MUSIC THEORY
PREPARATORY EXAM SET #1 - EXAM #4

7. a) Draw a line from each note to the rest with the same value.

b) Draw one note that is equal in value to the combined value of the given notes.

♪ ♪ ♪   = _____

𝅗𝅥 ♩   = _____

♩. ♪   = _____

♫   = _____

𝅗𝅥. ♩   = _____

♪ ♪   = _____

ULTIMATE MUSIC THEORY
PREPARATORY EXAM SET #1 - EXAM #4

8. a) Add bar lines to complete the following rhythms.

b) Add the correct Time Signature below each bracket.

ULTIMATE MUSIC THEORY
PREPARATORY EXAM SET #1 - EXAM #4

9. Circle the correct definition for each of the following signs or symbols.

Sign or Symbol	Definition		
f	soft	or	loud
mp	medium soft	or	medium loud
<	becoming louder	or	becoming softer
♯	lower the pitch of a note	or	raise the pitch of a note
mf	medium soft	or	medium loud
♩.	smooth	or	detached
>	becoming louder	or	becoming softer
p	soft	or	loud
♭	lower the pitch of a note	or	raise the pitch of a note
𝄐	detached	or	hold the note or rest longer than the written value

ULTIMATE MUSIC THEORY
PREPARATORY EXAM SET #1 - EXAM #4

10. Analyze the following excerpt of music by answering the questions below.

Aria in F Major

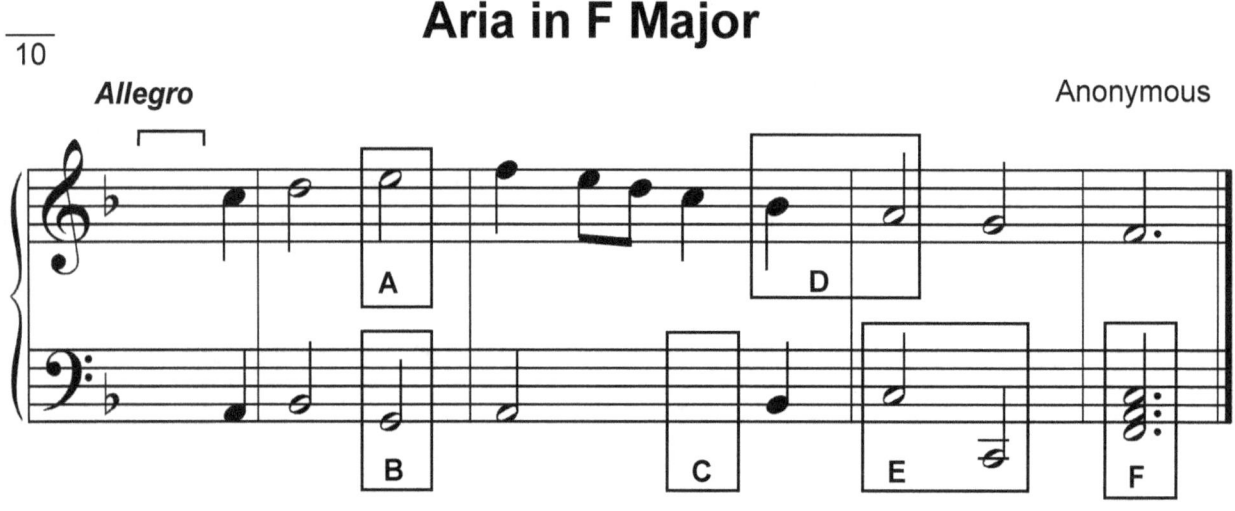

a) Name the title of this piece. _____

b) Explain the tempo of this piece. _____

c) Add the Time Signature directly on the music.

e) Name the notes at the letters **A**: _____ **B**: _____

d) Add the missing rest in the box at the letter **C**.

f) Name the interval at **D** (number size only). _____

g) Name the interval at **E** (number size only). _____

h) Circle the name of the triad at the letter **F**.   C Major   G Major   F Major

i) How many times does the note B♭ appear in this excerpt? _____

j) What is the lowest note in this piece? _____

ULTIMATE MUSIC THEORY EXAM SERIES

_____   _____

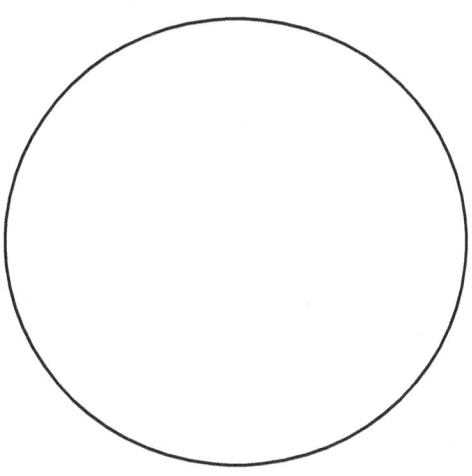

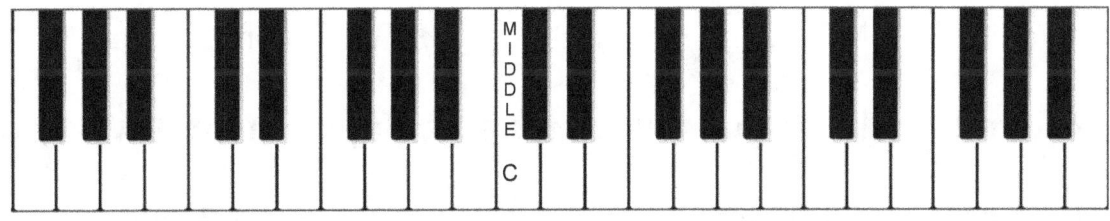

 UltimateMusicTheory.com © Copyright 2013 Gloryland Publishing. All Rights Reserved.

Workbooks, Exams, Answers, Online Courses, App & More!

A Proven Step-by-Step System to Learn Theory Faster - from Beginner to Advanced.

Innovative techniques designed to develop a complete understanding of music theory, to enhance sight reading, ear training, creativity, composition and musical expression.

All UMT Series have matching Answer Books!

The UMT Rudiments Series - Beginner A, Beginner B, Beginner C, Prep 1, Prep 2, Basic, Intermediate, Advanced & Complete (All-In-One)

- ♪ 12 Lessons, Review Tests, and a Final Exam to develop confidence
- ♪ Music Theory Guide & Chart for fast and easy reference of theory concepts
- ♪ 80 Flashcards for fun drills to dramatically increase retention & comprehension

Rudiments Exam Series - Preparatory, Basic, Intermediate & Advanced

- ♪ 8 Exams plus UMT Tips on How to Score 100% on Theory Exams

Each Rudiments Workbook correlates to a Supplemental Workbook.

The UMT Supplemental Series - Prep Level, Level 1, Level 2, Level 3, Level 4, Level 5, Level 6, Level 7, Level 8 & Complete (All-In-One) Level

- ♪ Form & Analysis and Music History - Composers, Eras & Musical Styles
- ♪ Melody Writing using ICE - Imagine, Compose & Explore
- ♪ 12 Lessons, Review Tests, Final Exam and 80 Flashcards for quick study

Supplemental Exam Series - Level 5, Level 6, Level 7 & Level 8

- ♪ 8 Exams to successfully prepare for nationally recognized Theory Exams

UMT Online Courses, Music Theory App & More

- ♪ UMT Certification Course, Teachers Membership & Elite Educator Program
- ♪ Ultimate Music Theory App correlates to the Rudiments Workbooks
- ♪ Free Resources - Teachers Guide, Music Theory Blogs, videos & downloads

Go To: **UltimateMusicTheory.com**